Foreign Policy and a State's Hierarchy of Needs: DOD and the New Security Strategy

Timothy P. Olwell

AIR WAR COLLEGE

AIR UNIVERSITY

FOREIGN POLICY AND A STATE'S HIERARCHY OF NEEDS: DoD AND THE NEW SECURITY STRATEGY

by

Timothy P. Olwell

Lieutenant Colonel, USAF

A PAPER SUBMITTED TO THE FACULTY

IN

FULFILLMENT OF THE CURRICULUM

REQUIREMENT

Advisor: Dr. Grant Hammond

MAXWELL AIR FORCE BASE, ALABAMA

March 1995

INTRODUCTION

The last 60 years saw a great change in United States involvement in the world. From an isolationist position before World War II, the United States moved to world leadership as underwriter of European security and balancer of Soviet expansionism. The reason this country bore the brunt of that huge undertaking was clear. It was in our "Vital National Interests." First, fascist aggression sought world domination, and war resulted. Then, the security of the United States was clearly tied to blocking the spread of communism through a national policy of containment. In November 1989, the Berlin Wall came tumbling down and with it Churchill's famous Iron Curtain. Just two years later, in December of 1991, the Union of Soviet Socialist Republics died. The rapid fall of the Soviet Communist regime did two drastic things to international politics. First, it ended the communist threat to the US and free world. Second, the fall ended the Cold War and with it, bipolarity. Now turbulence worldwide generates as ethnic and nationalistic sentiments surface and cause civil and regional conflicts. Previously, these sentiments were buried under the mantel of communism. These conflicts present new challenges for the world and those concerned with maintenance of its order. The United States has not determined how to define these problems and the interests of this country, nor what the proper response to these events should be. The old bipolar paradigm is inadequate and a new one must be developed. This paper proposes a new model for United States involvement around the world.

This daunting task was not undertaken lightly. The focus has shifted over time. The first topic for this paper was what strategy for arms control the United States should pursue in a post-START II environment. The difficulties inherent in that discussion led to

1

research of Air Force Doctrine and the problems with today's version. Although the current version is better than any previous one, it still does not provide the framework for either a post-START II discussion or a model for the future. The current doctrine still emphasizes full war and ignores most other missions or uses for the military forces short of military force.[1] Therefore, a search for a model explaining what this nation's interests were began. A model that would help define when military forces or force might be used began to emerge. The second trimester at the Air War College deals with National Security Decision Making and the readings for that course and ensuing discussions were pivotal in this study. This paper, then, focuses on this nation and its government's reaction to world events. What are the tradeoffs in a democracy when declaring events outside our border as a national interest? When do we commit military force or forces? This paper will try to develop a framework for analyzing international issues and events useful for arriving at a judgment on how important they are to United States national interests and when the DOD should become involved.

HIERARCHY OF NEEDS FOR A NATION-STATE

In 1954, Maslow developed a hierarchy of needs for the individual.[2] One of the things Maslow pointed out was the lower needs must be normally satisfied before an individual would work on higher level needs. Movement up or down the hierarchy is possible as time passes. For instance, an individual who has a good job and nice home may be working on level three or four items. However if he loses his job, a new priority will develop that may take him back down to level one. This would explain in our lives the ups and downs we experience as we move through time. It also explains a shift in

INDIVIDUAL HIERARCHY
OF NEEDS

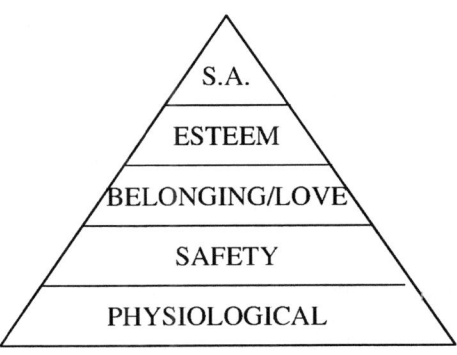

priorities from one year to the next. Maslow recognized that the order is not fixed. It

may vary slightly for different individuals. Also, he understood that there are relative

degrees of satisfaction. An individual could have a gradual emergence from one level to

another. He further stated that multiple motivations from several levels were possible for

the same act.[3]

    This led the me to think about a Hierarchy of Needs For a Nation-State. What are

the fundamental responsibilities of a government to its people and to other states? After

much study, I developed a Hierarchy of Needs For a Nation-State that looks like this:

NATIONAL HEIRACHY
OF NEEDS

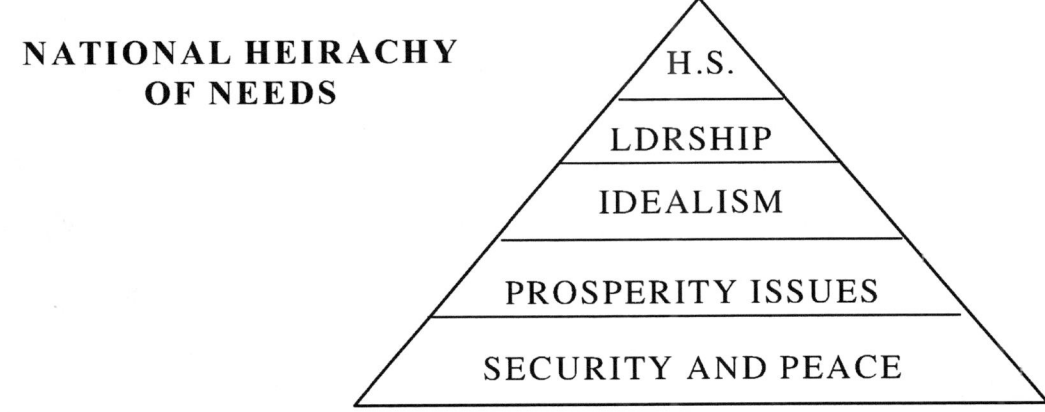

3

Maslow stated that you must first start at the bottom and ensure that level prior to moving up the individual Hierarchy. So it is with Nation-States.[4] The lowest level (level 1) is where a State must first concentrate its means and efforts. Security and Peace are a state's first and most critical concerns. The regime in power will want to guarantee the borders and existence of the government. Survival is included in this level. Years ago security may have been followed by Peace on the hierarchy. However, with the advent of nuclear weapons and the means to deliver them intercontinentally, for most states, security and peace have become intertwined. This level is a **Security National Interest.** It is easily understood by citizens and must be accomplished before expending efforts at the next level. Security National Interests enjoy popular support as they effect the majority of the population base. The President and the military establishment generally lead security issue debates. Very few others have the expertise, or access to required information, to influence the resources committed or to determine for what they are devoted to in a classic security issue.

The level for most central governments after security is Prosperity. Totalitarian regimes may seek to establish an Ideology second. Most regimes, though, will work on an increasing standard of living for itself and its people. Prosperity needs include economic development, education, infrastructure, trade agreements, standard of living, and health care. Another name for this level could be Quality of Life/Standard of Living. Working on this level does two important things for the regime in power. First, it enhances internal security by meeting expectations. This creates a situation where the government can take credit for an improving standard of living for its citizens. Second, a growing, prospering economy and electorate provides a broader base to draw resources from for level one and two efforts, and may allow policy pursuit in level three. Level two issues are of a **Vital National Interest** to a Nation-State. Vital means "of, pertaining to, or necessary to life."[5] Inside level two, many issues can compete for resources left over from level one activities. If the discussion is over education, local, state, and national policy makers will compete amongst themselves and against health care advocates for resource allocation.

Indeed, as you move up the hierarchy more and more experts in disparate fields can affect resource allocation and decision making. Unless the goal has broad public support, weighing these interests against one another is tricky business. If a state has resources left over or generated from success in prosperity issues, it may try to accomplish level three, Idealism, goals next.

Level three includes ideological goals for both inside and outside the country that the state may wish to pursue. These policies help define who the Nation-State is to itself and the world. Examples of this level in the domestic arena are universal suffrage, equal access for the handicapped, and civil rights. International examples for the United States are found in the 1995 National Security Strategy of Engagement and Enlargement. Issues such as free markets, promoting democracy and world trade agreements are covered by this level. Third World countries do not normally operate at this level. Poorer countries focus on security and development issues, and usually rely on other countries for support. In these cases, developing states concern themselves with security and vital interests. Idealistic issues are **Core National Interests**. 'Great Powers' operate at this level and higher. By traditional definition, Great Powers were states strong enough to successfully wage war without calling on allies. Great Powers are different than other states; they could only remain great if they were seen as willing and able to use force to acquire and protect even non-vital interests.[6] Great Powers have resources and foundations that allow them to export their way of life. They have status and prestige that make them sought after as allies or patrons or merely emulated for their success. Not all states will be able to or want to operate at a Great Power level and may not be concerned above level 1, 2, and internal level 3 issues.

Ideologies perform five functions for political entities. First, they provide a cognitive structure; a set of ideas that provide a basis for perceiving, understanding, and interpreting the world. For a state, a political ideology supplies a social constitution, a higher law. The second function is to provide a prescription for collective actions and judgments. The ideology justifies a society's allocation of scarce resources. By justifying the allocation, the ideology legitimizes the order. The third function of an ideology is to aid in conflict management. Ideology provides the code for an acceptable society. Fourth, ideology is an aid to self-identification. The ideology defines a state's being and foreshadows what it may become. Finally, an ideology provides a sense of purpose and commitment to action. It moves people to work, serve, and sacrifice.[7]

Committing resources after level two attainment is a luxury that allows the United States to work at the Idealism level. There are never "left over resources" for a modern state. Rather, there is a constant struggle for the amount, direction, and sustainment of both budgetary and political capital among competing interests. Historically, the US has decided to commit resources to this level and beyond. That is why the US can pursue core national interests. However, when those interests run up against a state that is working at level one or two, a disparity may develop over level of intensity of effort. A state at the lower level is liable to commit more resources to its security or vital issues than the US would against a core issue. This is where the Vietnam conflict fits in this model. A level three issue, Democracy, for a developed state may come into conflict with a level one issue, Civil War, in a developing one. This level, then, may be the dividing line on the hierarchical pyramid between developing and developed states. As states pursue external idealistic issues, they may vie for leadership on certain issues. Leadership is the next level on the pyramid.

Leadership may become important to some states that have met the first three rungs on the hierarchy and still have the political will to create or commit resources further. Resources are elastic and so is prestige. Some states may pursue world leadership on an issue. Others may stop at regional leadership or at level three. Leadership entails not only espousing ideals but providing the means for others to accomplish the ideals themselves. More than that though, prestige requires putting your own state resources at risk or spending them so others may follow your lead. Leadership is a **Peripheral National Interest**.

World leadership can be exercised towards policies on each level also. One state may lead in security issues in a region while another may lead in economic terms. A Great Power may attempt to lead on all levels including idealistic ones. To work on this level, the power base inside a country must be very secure and content. Otherwise, competition inside a country will not allow it to spend resources outside its borders. Since resource commitment is elastic, any drastic change in the state's fortunes or environment will cause a reappraisal of satisfaction at lower levels. This is why the US is struggling with health care and peacekeeping. Lower level satisfaction is critical prior to attempts at higher ones. The problem may not be the relative merits of programs, but resource availability in the current budget year cycle. Regional or world leadership attempts require a strong, secure country and a healthy, expanding economy.

The leadership role of a Great Power is a very important input for the other states but requires long term commitment from the sponsoring state. The United States participation in NATO and European security was such a commitment. Leadership on lower levels is easier to maintain than leadership at higher ones. For instance, regional stability or economic integration is easier to coordinate than support for intervention in a civil war.

Once a state gains regional or world leadership on an issue, maintenance of that leadership position may take on significance. Loss of national prestige may be a vital or core national interest. As a state moves up and down the ladder, it redefines itself causing shifting expectations in politicians and the populace. Moving up the pyramid brings recognition and prestige along with the increased resources committed. Gratification on a certain level may not necessarily equate to happiness, but loss of it on another level will cause great disharmony. Moving down the pyramid is hard to accept after losing your former position of leadership and the government still wants to have a preeminent part in world affairs. "A state such as the United States that has achieved international primacy has every reason to attempt to maintain that primacy through peaceful means so as to preclude the need to have to fight a war to maintain it."[8] This may also be true for Great Britain and Russia. If world leadership is successful at the lower levels, the state may wish to commit resources to work on the final one, human sovereignty.

Human Sovereignty (H.S.) may be the nation-states equivalent to "self-actualization." Boutros Boutros-Ghali uses the term "Human Sovereignty." Jefferson called this "Inalienable Rights." Rousseau called it "Natural Rights." Former President Carter called this simply "Human Rights." In the Declaration of Independence in 1776, Jefferson wrote "We hold these truths to be self evident, that all men are created equal, that they are endowed by their Creator with certain inalienable rights, that among these are Life, Liberty and the Pursuit of Happiness." That Declaration has helped shape this country for over 200 years. Issues like these link with humanity and not just local nationalism. They deal with the human condition. Each person has a stake in the earth's future and a right to some share of the world's riches. This level has been attempted only a few times in the history of the world.[9] Human Sovereignty goals are a **Supra National Interest**. Nation-States may have to approach the level of "Empire" or have the cooperation of a UN type confederation to have enough resources to simultaneously work all five levels at once. As a minimum, world security and peace among developed states would have to be achieved or underwritten as a precondition for pursuing goals at this level.. Developed states would have to strive for that circumstance. Once each state knows it will survive and regimes can divert resources away from defense spending, worldwide progress will be easier. Level five issues are Supra National Issues for all states leading towards their accomplishment. Linkage of level five issues to other states' lower levels will be important for the state trying to lead. Through linkage, a Great Power may entice states to divert resources to problems that otherwise would not be worked. For instance, by underwriting elections abroad, this country may help a state towards democracy that does not have an economic base to pay for the infrastructure

9

required for the electoral process. As this country set up the election, it could enact universal suffrage enhancing the human rights of the people in the lesser developed country. Like individuals, states may function best when they strive for something that makes them stand out from others, or defines them.

Higher needs rely more on a favorable environment (outside conditions). Just as an individual may require a good neighborhood for safety and a well-adjusted family for belonging, a state relies on its neighbors and allies to help define the limits of what is attainable. Higher needs are less imperative than security. As such, they are less urgent than lower ones. The higher the level of the need, the more preconditions to attempting policies aimed at it. These higher needs, ideals, are what give life meaning and purpose. They may not be rational, attainable, or universal, but they do motivate individuals, peoples and governments. Capable leaders must be able to generate resources to pursue these national or supra national interests.

NATIONAL INTEREST HIERARCHY

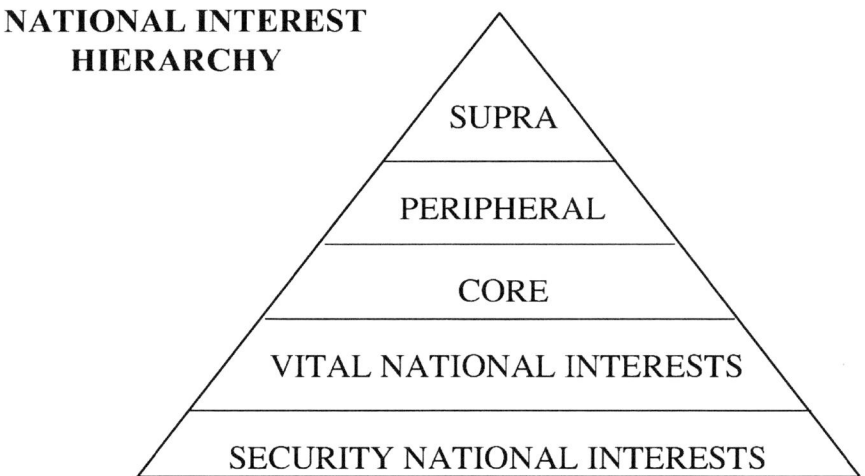

In the explanation of each NEEDS level, a type of National Interest involved was mentioned. Each level involves all elements of national power to some extent. However,

Security National Interests are issues for which a State will almost always be willing to use military force, even if that use was as a last resort. Threats to Vital National Interests will always cause states to consider the use of military force. Issues involving Core National Interests will sometimes cause consideration of the use of military force. States primarily pursue core policies with other instruments of national power. The attainment of Peripheral National Interests will almost never rely on military force to achieve leadership. They may require some use of military power to work the issue on which we are trying to lead. For instance, military force would not be used to set up a coalition but would be part of the coalition strategy. Supra National Issues may require use of military force in situations where a functioning government ceases to function or exist. But, interested states cannot solve this type of problems with military force where a functioning government does exist.

If the level five state introduces military force into another state to enforce a humanitarian issue, the invaded state now has a level one issue on its hands. The security level was a mass mobilizer in many instances around the world. The breach of sovereignty is a more serious threat to the lower state. Usually, the security concern is the strongest motivator, the strongest will. In addition, the will at the supra national level is usually at its weakest. The use of force will not allow for a cooperative working of the level five issue.

Military force is usually involved in level one to three issues only. Military personnel, vice military force, can be used to further national interests at any level in a cooperative venture with the other states involved. Entry of military forces has to be agreed to ahead of time or it is a forcible entry. Forcible entry is employment of military force rather than the deployment of military forces (personnel).

Now the discussion turns from the Hierarchy of Needs for a Nation-State, levels of National Interests, and when the military instrument of national power might be used, to the discussion of how the National Security Decision Making Process in this country works.

POLICY TO STRATEGY BOX

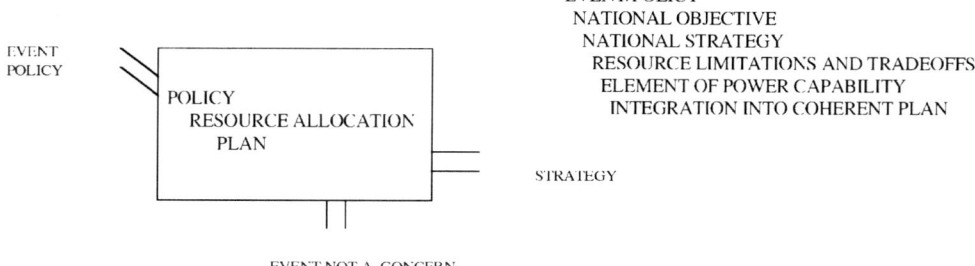

The policy to strategy process in the United States is issue dependent. An event (Reactive-Engagement) or policy (Proactive-Enlargement) triggers a debate inside the Policy to Strategy Box. As an issue arises, the event or policy is the input that causes activation of the decision making process inside the box. Depending on the issue, the number of players will vary, as will the composition of the group. A real and immediate threat to our sovereignty or an ally's, or to American lives, will limit the number of participants as a decision forms rapidly. This type of policy to strategy decision is primarily one dealing with a Security National Interest and may simply be a decision to execute a preplanned strategy. If the event was unforeseen, the output from the box will be the strategy to deter or defeat the threat to our Security. As the Issue entering the box gets higher up the Hierarchy of Needs pyramid, the time allotted to the process grows, as does the number of players.

As the time to decide a policy to strategy debate grows, the competing interests at the State's Hierarchy of Needs level come forward. In a nation-state, everyone has a stake in the security issues. Rallying public support on these issues is relatively easy. As the issue becomes Vital or Core, regional differences inside a country, interest group competition and competition for scarce resources may increase the time needed to reach consensus on the solutions considered. In addition, time allows for the debate on what is the most important goal at a given level. The constituency for domestic agenda items will be hard to overcome for international idealism agenda items. Nevertheless, the input will start the political process moving and the debate will take place.

For this paper, it is important to realize that the satisfaction of each level and graduation to the next may not have national agreement. While Americans in Iowa may feel perfectly secure with the demise of the Soviet Union, those living in south Florida may feel an immigration threat to their way of life. Another example is the uneven economic opportunity across this country. In the growing west, prospects for prosperity seem different form somewhere in the Northeast where the only plant in town may have just closed. Where you stand on an issue depends both on where and how you live (populace) and where you live (leadership). Education and welfare are also locality and station in life dependent. National issues may enjoy general support notwithstanding local pockets of discontent.

Potential discontent is important because people are important in a democracy. Local representatives will work to ensure the individual's level on Maslow's Hierarchy is as high as possible before the Member of Congress will work to hard on the national scale above level two. In addition, a policy that is seen to be level three in some areas of the country may be seen to be level two in the area the policy is aimed towards. It is not always clear cut and some issues bleed from one level to another. Slavery was seen as an idealistic issue in the north and an economic or survival issue in the south. This discussion is important because states spend their limited resources to attain satisfaction at each level before attempting a National Interest at the next level.

Attaining resources necessary to pursue higher policy goals is a very complex process. If there are no resources to commit after attainment of national level two, level three issues have to wait. Obviously, there are forms of national power that do not require great expenditures of funds. Most do require some form of capital and even good will is finite. In a democracy, leadership usually spends resources with the consent of the taxpayer. That consent is not always by a wide margin. In a democracy, the support is more often 51-49 %, not 80-20%. 60 % of the vote in an election is a landslide (20% differential). If the leadership gets it wrong, or the support changes, there are slow and complex feedback loops with forward and backward linkages. This process is heavily personality dependent and fragile. Hence, there is discussion on how will this be seen in Peoria or Lubbock? The ability to decide amongst competing social, economic, domestic and international ills and apportion scarce resources is becoming more difficult. The richer you are as a state, the more lax you can be about the policies you pursue. The more the government involves itself across the country or the world, the more it spends resources. If the resources do not stretch far enough, peripheral issues are either dropped or redefined. A level three and four issue, such as leadership on Non Proliferation, may have to wait until it becomes a level one threat to successfully compete for funding. The case of North Korea is an illustration of this.

Once the event enters the Box, the group, unwittingly or not, decides whether it is a Security, Vital, Core, Peripheral, or Supra national issue. Depending on what level it is at or labeled, different agencies will have the lead or preeminent strategy development role. If the event does not match up against one of our interests, the issue should drop out of the bottom. Under the new National Security Strategy of "Engagement and Enlargement," more and more events around the world will stimulate some response from the United States. This will require proactive planning and resource allocation for new capabilities.

If an event is determined to be a security issue, DOD may have preeminence during the policy debate. Department of State follows closely behind. The decision maker will be the President. The National Military Strategy of the United States provides guidance on where, when, and with what means, the armed forces will conduct campaigns. These issues are usually not as contentious as the rest. The higher you go on the ladder, the more contentious the debate and the less the DOD plays in the decision making process. For instance, DOD has little to say on prosperity issues except through levels of procurement Congress authorizes. Some dual-use technology is created but that has not been a primary concern of DOD in the past. The paradigm shift occurred too recently to create good plans and commit resources to strategies for the non-security/economic issues the US is pursuing today. The Presidential leadership style is important for other goals as well as security.

The president can use one of three leadership styles. Collegial, competitive, or formal are the three outlined by Alexander George.[10] The style will decide who is allowed to enter the decision making process when the issue is inside or outside the normal purview of their portfolios. Also, the leadership style of the President will impact the support, cohesiveness, and implementation of the strategy after committal of resources. In the collegial style, anyone with access to the President can make formal or informal, on-line or off-line, inputs on issues even remotely affecting their normal responsibility areas. This is especially true if the discussion lasts very long. As resources are being discussed, more and more suggestions for better ways to spend the diverted funds will arise. Requests will take flight that had been grounded previously waiting for an opportunity to be funded. This type of style can lead to gridlock, policy turnabouts and poor outside support for the decision. This is especially true if the issue is one of enlargement and the strategy is a long term commitment and down the road attainment of success.

The competitive style has departments compete for influence and resources in an adversarial role. Through this open debate, the President can sit back and await a consensus or decision. The process creates a winner and loser and undermines some support. However, since views were discussed and the decision made openly, some attention by the President towards the loser can ensure no hurt feelings and public support. In the competitive model, there is always the next time.

The formal model utilizes a structured environment for players, agenda and access. If you are privy to the discussion, your input will be welcome and weighed. If not invited in, your input is not welcome. This system of Presidential leadership requires the policy advocate to be on the inside to be effective. Once out of an issue, you are marginalized and may be left out of the next debate. The Chief of Staff at the White House has a very important role in policy making by closely controlling access to the President during debate and decision making times. Support can be hard to generate among those left outside the process.

These three models further complicate the knowledge required to be able to predict the output of the policy to strategy process. The level of immediacy and the amount of wide spread support generated will allow the President greater latitude. As the interest is higher on the pyramid and the time frame shifts to long term benefit, the President loses sole control of the decision and it becomes a drive for consensus. The big debates may not be on what, but on how. The policy may be agreed upon and potential strategy clear. In today's environment, the resource allocation or reallocation is the tough part. The tradeoffs for an increased DOD budget may be the downfall of the issue over the idea. Bureaucratic politics and group interactions will play a huge role in the what and how decisions at level 2 and higher debates.

With this discussion of the complexity of the decision making box and the prior one on interests, the basis for the model is complete. Each individual is making choices, great and small, that cumulatively determine the kind of person he becomes- So it is with a state. Now we will turn to some historical data for a look at how the US is developing as a state.

HISTORICAL EXAMPLES

INDIVIDUAL

NATIONAL NEEDS

NATIONAL INTERESTS

```
        S.A.
      ESTEEM
   BELONGING LOVE            H.S.
      SAFETY             LDRSHIP          SUPRA
    PHYSIOLOGICAL        IDEALISM
                         PROSPERITY      PERIPHERAL
                    SECURITY AND PEACE     CORE
                                          VITAL
                                         SECURITY
```

The strength of a model is how well it can help describe, explain and ultimately, predict. One way to assess this is to look at how well a model explains the past. Since paradigm shifts mean something has changed, reliance on being able to explain the past is not a complete validation of a model to predict the future. Comparison of the past can lend credibility if the previous paradigm was too limited or wrong. The Cold War paradigm was limited and something has changed. A historical look is a partial attempt to give credibility to this model. Since the bi-polar Cold War power relationship started after W.W.II, that is where this check will start.

Peace in 1945 found this country in an enviable position as the world's sole remaining economic power. The vast destruction around the world had a devastating effect where the war occurred. However, the war created and spared a giant engine of mass production in this country. That yielded excess resources for the pursuit of interests above level 2. First, the Marshall plan resupplied Europe for food stuffs and self defense. These decisions were level 5 (prevent starvation), level 4 (ensure US could influence post world stability), level 3 (promote democratic institutions and free market economies), level 2 (ensure further markets for our domestic output), and level 1 (prevent the need to straighten out Europe a third time in the 20th Century). The Marshall Plan is an example of Maslow's multiple motivations.

The President therefore was able to create a Security, Vital, Core, Peripheral, and Supra National Interest out of the Marshall Plan. Truman said in 1955 of the Marshall Plan

> "This ... was something new in the history of nations. The traditional practice had always been for the conqueror to strip the defeated countries to make off with whatever spoils were available. Our idea has been to restore conquered nations ... to prosperity in the hope that they would understand the futility of aggression as a means of expansion and progress. [11]

It won support and succeeded over time because of the collegial but strong leadership of Truman.

Another instance in history that will shed light on the National Security Decision Making in this country is the Vietnam War policy under President Johnson. Johnson was not convinced of the expertise of the military. He was making decisions in his Tuesday lunches without much input from the military on bombing targets. Johnson also believed this was not a security or vital interest of this nation but an idealistic one. His Great Society program was a level two national interest in his eyes and Vietnam was a level three interest. Johnson was not willing to forego his social agenda for the war effort and this country tried to buy both guns and butter.

The Nixon administration followed Johnson. President Nixon saw the growing

arms race as a level 1 issue and the opening of China as a level 1 and 2 issue. By

exploiting the split between China and the Soviet Union, US security could be enhanced.

In addition, opening of Chinese markets would have a huge effect on our economy. He

wanted to work on these two problems and rid himself of the divisive Vietnam War as an

international and domestic issue. The war was in the way. Nixon worked to solve the

bipolar foundation seen for the war, reduce expenditures on the arms race, and open the

Chinese market to help divide the communist world and further US commerce. This

culmination of policies intertwined around the Vietnam War were level 1 through 4.

Nixon was able to craft a "Peace with Honor" exit from South East Asia by making it an

Ideological goal rather than a Security one. If it was an Ideal to have a free South

Vietnam and the South was free when we left, we achieved our goal. If the Security of

this nation rested on a free and independent South Vietnam, then clearly we later lost that

interest. However you judge Nixon, he was able to get past an inherited issue (level 1 or 3

depending on your view point) and work on level 1 through 4 issues.

President Carter wanted to work level 3, 4 and 5 issues. He was strongly in favor

of linking all foreign policy issues to advances in Human rights. This policy linked

idealism, leadership, and an attempt towards world human rights. He created a standard

for acceptable behavior for states. In 1977, President Carter said

> We have no wish to tell other nations what political or social system they should have,
> but we want our own worldwide influence to reduce human suffering and not to increase
> it. We are therefore working to advance a whole range of human rights--economic and
> social as well as political. [12]

In 1980 he went on to say "Our security is tied to human rights and social justice

prevailing among other people on earth."[13] He was unable to pursue this policy because the cold war was not over and security issues forced the US to ignore certain idealistic issues for pragmatic defense ones. Carter finally recognized the problem with the Soviet Union when it invaded Afghanistan. His Human Rights crusade was a victim of that war thousands of miles from the White House. He had trouble finding consensus on levels 3, 4, and 5 because 1 and 2 were not acknowledged in this country as being satisfied. Carter's level 3, 4, and 5 goals were victims of level 1 uncertainty.

Carter was also a victim of Reagan's "Pain Index." The Pain Index was a level 2 election issue. Adding the inflation rate and the unemployment rate gave the politicians a pain index. Reagan capitalized on his "Evil Empire" theme at the level 1 and Pain Index at the level 2 national interest to win a resounding victory over an incumbent President. His ability to get large defense budgets approved was a result of his mastery of framing the Security National interest at stake. He was successful as the "Great Communicator." He provided simple contexts for framing his vision of the path the nation should take. Through his vision, he was able to get the public support for many of his programs that carried the day in Congress.

Security issues were still important at the start of President Bush's term. However, the end of the Cold War and the Presidential Nuclear Initiatives brought a realization that level 1 issues for the United States and our Allies could now be more easily taken for granted. Bush was careful to craft a "Just War" reasoning for the Desert Shield/Storm operation and war. This was a level 2 and 3 national interest. He was the first President free of the bipolar baggage and was able to successfully use the cold war military to defeat a third world aggressor. Bush lost sight of level 2 desires in the populace who were tired of their sacrifices to underwrite security around the world. President Clinton was able to effectively capitalize on this feeling with his slogan in the 1992 campaign of "It's the Economy, Stupid."[14] Bush clearly lost sight of the level 2 issues and used resources for level 3 items when many in this country worried about level 2.

President Clinton inherited a world perceived with small level one issues for the United States and a relatively good position in level 2. He has outlined policies clearly in the level 3 area both domestically and internationally. He has not come to grips with when use of military power is appropriate at each level of the Hierarchy of Needs. His desire to approach level 3 and beyond issues will be contingent on his creating a strong political base that agrees that this country is doing well in prosperity programs. After all, he ran on that platform. In addition, he must make careful selections between domestic and international level 3 issues. Miscalculations between level 2 satisfaction and the correct level 3 policies to pursue may have resulted in the dramatic loss of the democratic majority in the House and Senate in the 1994 national elections. The point for this essay is that national consensus on level 3 or beyond issues is hard to create and even harder to sustain.

The historical examples tried to tie together the Hierarchy on Needs for Nation-States, Level of National Interest, use of Military force, and policy making. They were not intended to highlight partisan issues. The critical point is that the military has primary responsibility for level 1 and today the American populace worries about level 2 and 3 issues. How should the DOD respond? A look at past doctrines for insight follows.

A LOOK AT AMERICA'S DOCTRINES

The Bill of Rights could be considered one of America's first Doctrines. It dealt primarily with internal issues but laid the foundation to the world of what the fledgling nation thought was important. It laid out the ideals that the United States would strive to achieve. The first ten amendments were clearly to protect this experiment of democracy and to protect the individual from his government. Those are level 1 and 3 issues.

The next form of National Doctrine came in 1823 with the Monroe Doctrine. It banned European colonization in the American continents in the future. The level 1 issue was to keep the European interests and US interests from clashing and to promote a chance for self determination in the Americas, a level 3 issue. The Monroe Doctrine also was a leadership statement for the US in this hemisphere.

Another expression of level 3 and 4 issues in a doctrinal format was Wilson's 14 points. The United States had just participated in World War 1 and Wilson was concerned with the capability of the international system to prevent another world war. The 14 points were to create a joint effort among nations to secure level 1 rights and security so all states could concentrate on level 2 and higher interests. The United States could not get past its level 2 interests and the 14 points died. They were a reflection of growing concern of level 3 and above interests and the United States place in achieving a better world.

Wilson was right that the world needed mechanisms to prevent a second world war. Roosevelt laid out his doctrine for entering that war with his Four Freedoms Speech in 1941. In it he said, "We look forward to a world founded upon four essential freedoms ... freedom of speech and expression ... freedom of every person to worship God in his own way ... freedom from want ... freedom from fear."[15]   Roosevelt listed these as

reasons to join the war and commit United States treasure and youth to the effort. The

attack on Pearl Harbor gave the effort a level 1 reason and his four freedoms speech gave

it a higher calling. Whether they are level 3, 4 or 5 is not certain but they are a great

expression of a higher goal than fighting back aggression against the United States.

The Truman Doctrine built on the four freedoms speech when President Truman

stated in 1947,

> Totalitarian regimes imposed upon free peoples, by direct or indirect aggression,
> undermine the foundations of international peace and hence the security of the United
> States ... It must be the policy of the United States to support free peoples who are
> resisting attempted subjugation by armed minorities or by outside pressures ... I believe
> that our help should be primarily through economic and financial aid which is essential
> to economic stability and orderly political processes.[16]

This is a clear enunciation by Truman of level 3 issues and level 4 leadership. He also

realized that those issues were best achieved not through military means but by other uses

of national power. Apparently he knew dealing on this level meant committing American

funds for the accomplishment of Core and Peripheral National Interests.

Another example of an American doctrine is the Carter Doctrine. In it President

Carter tied the health of the American Economy with the stability of the Persian Gulf

region and free access to oil. During his State of the Union address in January 1980,

Carter said:

> Let our position be absolutely clear: an attempt by any outside force to gain control of
> the Persian Gulf region will be regarded as an assault on the vital interests of the United
> States of America. And such an assault will be repelled by any means necessary,
> including military force.

This was a clear tying of level 1 issues of our allies and a level 2 issue of the United

States. It also was a basis for the Desert Storm/Shield operation a decade later.

The American Doctrines have helped define what level of National Interest was at stake during different periods of our history. They also served to create long term policy interests validated through the policy to strategy box. Many resulted in on the shelf military responses to challenges to them. The public statement of the doctrines allowed the resource debate to build and consensus to form behind them. They further defined for ourselves, and the world, who we were and for what we stood. Kennedy's 1961 "pay any price, bear any burden to assure the survival and success of liberty" speech[17] was tantamount to announcing to the world the US engagement for the long run. President Clinton, who has said he was greatly influenced by President Kennedy, is just building on that speech with his policy of "Engagement and Enlargement." Now this country has to work out when to use the military and when to use other instruments of power without military force.

IMPLICATIONS FOR THE DOD

The DOD must frame issues for the winning of this nation's war in level 1 and 3 terms. DOD can use level 3 issues to reinforce level 1 success. As already stated, DOD has little influence on level 2 issues in this country. Congress decides the shape of the budget and how much is industrial base or procurement committed. DOD can, however, shape budget requests along these lines with a basis in level 1 future needs. In addition, DOD must fully explore and support those level 3 issues that help keep this country above level 1 fights. For instance, Non-Proliferation and Counter-Proliferation of Weapons of Mass Destruction are in the level 3, 4 and level 1 interest of the United States. Therefore, DOD should quickly adopt these national concerns and create capabilities to attain them.

Other level 3 issues are harder to directly link to level 1 issues. However, anything that continues to make local or regional access available to US military forces is in DOD's interest. This may mean Mobile Training Teams, International Military Education and Training, or Corps of Engineer assistance. It could also be port calls by the US Navy with time built in to create playgrounds at school yards or conduct field health clinics. These things are clearly level 3 or higher issues with level 1 implications. DOD needs to create opportunities to get linkage between level 2 and higher issues to preserve a level 1 capability. DOD should look to provide service people and expertise to help higher issues while reserving military force for defense of level 1 and 2 issues.

The United States military establishment alone in the government contains core competencies that other branches do not. These include organization with strong command and control, communication networks across this country and the world, transportation and mobility, and logistics support in the field. These core competencies are what DOD can offer the decision maker in using military forces, but not military force, in a situation.

DOD must enlarge its scope of opportunities to help the national decision makers. The USMC with it's "911 force" is seen to do this. It is time the other services, and DOD as a whole, come up with adaptive force packages that tailor already paid for capabilities to answer national concerns. The taxpayers have purchased DOD core competencies and they should be able to call on them when needed. The President decides when that is, not DOD. Being in on the decision making process will allow DOD to help shape when and what competencies the President uses. DOD can only survive by being engaged in an enlarged arena.

CONCLUSION

This paper proposed a model to help form a new paradigm for conducting defense debates. It started with a discussion of a Hierarchy of Needs for a Nation-State. Remember a state can rise and fall on the hierarchy as easily as an individual can. Regional arms races or natural disasters can create new situations that divert resources from higher purposes. That can happen to the United States also. Developing states, like minimum wage workers, are only one "hiccup" away from level 1 at any time. After that, a discussion of National Interest categories followed to help tie the thought of consensus problems to National Interest levels. The primacy of the military in level 1 issues was also introduced to show lack of dominance at other levels. Then, the Policy to Strategy Box discussion showed how many varied inputs and agendas might impact policy formulation. Bureaucratic politics were briefly discussed on level 2 and higher issues. Outlining resource allocation problems emphasized current budget realities.

Next, I looked at historical examples and American Doctrines to help assess the robustness of this model. The model may help the new paradigm develop. This country is in a state of identity crisis and internal change. As Americans redefine themselves, and decide what level of needs they take for granted, they will move up and down the pyramid, until they find the correct level of national interest to work.

As they search for that position, resources will be key. What price are Americans willing to pay to impact change around the world? Is our vision of ourselves contracting? This situation will only exacerbate with continued deficit concerns or balanced budget pressures. The American people are getting more stingy with their tax dollars. This brings back the point out that DOD has to help the decision maker in level 2 and above issues to remain a viable participant in the box at levels above level 1. DOD must prepare to use its core competencies to help the President solve problems. Otherwise, DOD risks a dwindling resource base and disaster in the future when called upon to handle level 1 threats.

The model hopefully will give the reader a context to look at any situation, any event around the world or long term policy goal of any administration, and predict in gross terms public support and military response. It will take thought to know what level of need this country and others are at. It is not a given. The levels change rapidly. The correct packaging of a problem may place it in the right level of interest. Only after identifying the correct national interest should the discussion of use of military forces or force be undertaken. Finally, policy makers must correctly identify the proper resources, appropriate objectives, craft a workable strategy and then plan and execute our policy accordingly.

I offer this model to help assess where this nation is, on what level a situation exists, and what modifiers go in front of the much abused term "national interest." By correctly identifying the problem and the adjective for national interest, decision makers can properly address military involvement in the solution. DOD must be ahead of this debate so it can help properly place the problem at the right level of national need. Then, decision makers will know what level of national interest is at stake. Once known, they may select military force or forces to help craft a solution. With that input, the President can look at the tradeoffs involved. DOD must make sure he is aware of the costs. To do that, DOD must be inside the process, actively seeking to help create a solution. DOD must start today to reorient itself to be able to offer solution sets for level 1, 2, and 3

problems. If the services wait, others will create solutions without them. This could lead

potentially to the wrong use of force or forces, the wrong cost-benefit analysis, and the

wrong tradeoffs being made. This could lead to disaster for future level 1 defense

capability. DOD must prepare to be "engaged and enlarged." This model should help

start that process.

---

[1] Air Force Manual 1-1, March 1992.

[2] Maslow, A. H., Motivation and Personality, Harper and Row, New York, 1954.

[3] Ibid. Discussion is in chapter two.

[4] For another opinion, see Arnold, Edwin J., "The Use of Military Power in Pursuit of National Interests," The National Interest, Summer 1992, pp. 56-62.

[5] Random House College Dictionary, Random House Inc., NY, 1975, p. 1472.

[6] Luttwak, Edward N., "Where are all the Great Powers?", Foreign Affairs, July 1994, pp. 23-28.

[7] Christenson, et al., Ideologies and Modern Politics, Harper and Row, NY, 1981. This paragraph summarizes pp. 12-15.

[8] Huntington, Samuel P., "Why International Primacy Matters," International Security, Spring 1993, p 70. I chose the word leadership over primacy because leadership entails cooperative efforts, not coercive. The US strives to lead on the basis of opportunity more than fear.

[9] An example of this might be the Marshall plan following World War Two. The United States' concern over the starving and needs of the people of Europe among other concerns led to a massive underwriting of European recovery. Foodstuffs and the ability to produce them were of primary concern. Our self-interest was also at stake as European states had been among our largest trading partners.

[10] George, Alexander, Presidential Decision-Making in Foreign Policy, Weatview Press, Boulder, CO, 1980.

[11] Miller and Sargent, compilers, From George ... to George, 200 years of Presidential Quotations, Braddock Communications, 1989, p. 100.

[12] Ibid., p. 66.

[13] Ibid., p. 67

[14] Morris, Charles R., "It's Not the Economy, Stupid", The Atlantic Monthly, July 1993, pp. 49-62.

[15] Miller, p. 13.

[16] Ibid., p. 13.

[17] Ibid., p. 14.

BIBLIOGRAPHY

ARTICLES

Abrams, Elliot, "Why America Must Lead," The National Interest, Summer 1992, pp. 56-62.

Arnold, Edwin J., "The Use of Military Power in Pursuit of National Interests," Parameters, Spring 1994, pp.4-12.

Bond, Brian, "Limited Liability or No Liability at All," chapter in British Military between the Two World Wars, Oxford University Press, 1980, pp. 244-286.

Boyd, Lt Gen and Lt Col Westenhoff, "Air Power Thinking: Request Unrestricted Climb," Airpower Journal, Fall 1991, pp. 4-15.

Baker, James A., III, "Selective Engagement," Vital Speeches, 1 Mar 1994, pp. 299-302.

Clarke, Arthur C., "Superiority," Reprinted with permission in NSS Book 2, AWC, AU, 1994, pp. 37-46.

Cohen, Eliot A., "The Mystique of US Airpower," Foreign Affairs, Jan 1994, pp. 109-124.

Coll, Alberto R., "Power, Principles, and Prospects for a Cooperative International Order," Washington Quarterly, Winter 1993, pp. 5-14.

Estep, Lt Col David G., "Air Mobility: The Strategic Use of Nonlethal Airpower," Unpublished Master's thesis, SAAS, AU, 1994.

Foster, Gregory D., "America and the World: A Security Agenda for the Twenty-First Century," Strategic Review, Spring 1993, p.. 20-29.

Hitt, Jack, et al, "Forum: Is there a Doctrine in the House?" Harper's Magazine, Jan 1994, pp. 57-64.

Huntington, Samuel P., "Why International Primacy Matters," International Security, Spring 1993, pp. 68-83.

Jordan, Amos, Taylor and Korb, "The Role of the Military in the National Security Policy Process," American National Security, 1993, pp. 164-188.

Kenichi, Ohmae, "The Rise of the Region State," Foreign Affairs, Spring 1993, pp. 78-87.

Klare, Michael T., "The New Challenges to Global Security," <u>Current History</u>, April 1993, pp. 155-161.

Lake, Anthony, "From Containment to Enlargement: Current Foreign Policy Debates in perspective," <u>Vital Speeches</u>, 15 Oct 1993, pp. 13-19.

Luttwak, Edward N., "Where are the Great Powers," <u>Foreign Affairs</u>, July 1994, pp. 23-28.

McCain, Senator John, "Preserving International Stability in the Post-Cold War Era," <u>Strategic Review</u>, Summer 1993, pp. 7-19.

Miller, ADM P. D., "Both Swords and Plowshares: Military Roles in the 1990s," <u>RUSI Journal</u>, April 1993, pp. 13-19.

Morris, Charles R., "It's Not the Economy, Stupid," <u>The Atlantic Monthly</u>, July 1993, pp.49-62.

Novak, Vicca, "The Long Brawl," <u>National Journal</u>, 8 Jan 1994, Pp. 58-62.

Owens, ADM William A., "JROC: Harnessing the Revolution in Military Affairs," <u>Joint Force Quarterly</u>, Summer 1994, pp. 55-57.

Patullo, E. L., "War and the American Press," <u>Parameters</u>, Winter 1992-3, pp. 61-69.

Smith, Tony, "In Defense of Intervention," <u>Foreign Affairs</u>, Nov 1994, pp. 34-46.

Zakem and Ranney, "Matching Defense Strategies to Resources: Challenges for the Clinton Administration," <u>International Security</u>, Summer 1993, pp. 51-78.

BOOKS

Builder, Carl A., <u>The Icarus Syndrome</u>, Transaction Publishers, New Brunswick, NJ, 1993.

Bullock, Alan, <u>The Fontana Dictionary of Modern Thought</u>, Fontana Books, Great Britain, 1983.

Christenson, et al, <u>Ideologies and Modern Politics</u>, Harper and Row, NY, 1981.

George, Alexander, <u>Presidential Decision-Making in Foreign Policy</u>, Weatview Press, Boulder, Co, 1980.

Holley, I. B., <u>Ideas and Weapons</u>, Office of Air Force History, 1983.

Jordan, Amos A., et al, <u>American National Security</u>, John Hopkins University Press, Baltimore, 1990.

Maslow, Abraham H., <u>Motivation and Personality</u>, Harper and Row, NY, 1987.

Miller and Sargent, compilers, <u>From George to George, 200 years of Presidential Quotations</u>, Braddock Communications, 1989.

Paret, Peter, editor, <u>Makers of Modern Strategy</u>, Princeton University Press, NJ, 1986.

Spangler, Stanley E., <u>Force and Accommodation in World Politics</u>, AU Press, AL, 1991.

Warden, Col John, <u>The Air Campaign; Planning for Combat</u>, NDU Press, Wash , DC, 1988.

PAMPHLETS

<u>Air Force Manual 1-1,</u> March 1992.

<u>A National Security Strategy of Engagement and Enlargement, July 1994</u>, US Gov Printing Office.

<u>Jt Pub 1, Joint Warfare of the US Armed Forces</u>, Nov 1991.

CPSIA information can be obtained at www.ICGtesting.com
Printed in the USA
BVOW06s1414111113

336012BV00013B/484/P